IT IS WRITTEN...
MY VOICE IN VERSES

A POET'S PERSPECTIVE

YVETTE Y. CARTER

PUBLISHED BY
THIS IS WHY, INC.
ARLINGTON, VA

IT IS WRITTEN...MY VOICE IN VERSES:
A POET'S PERSPECTIVE
COPYRIGHT 2021 YVETTE Y. CARTER

PUBLISHED BY: THIS IS WHY, INC.
2300 NORTH PERSHING DRIVE
SUITE 356
ARLINGTON, VA 22201

COVER DESIGN AND FORMATTING: **LSDdesign**
CONTEXT AND COPY EDITING:
DARCELLA PERKINS, KINITE MCCRAE, JENNIFER WESTBROOK

PRINTED IN THE UNITED STATES OF AMERICA

IT IS WRITTEN...MY VOICE IN VERSES: A POET'S PERSPECTIVE
ISBN: 978-1-7328129-3-2 - PAPERBACK
ISBN: 978-1-7328129-6-3 - KINDLE EBOOK

TABLE OF CONTENTS

ACKNOWLEDGMENTS AND DEDICATIONS

This book is dedicated to my mother, Bertha M. Coleman. She was strength, peace, kindness and love for me. I miss her so much. I did it, Mommy!

For my big brother Kevin, I still can't believe you are not here with me to celebrate this moment. I know you are smiling down from heaven. Your voice is in my head and your memory is in my heart. Gone suddenly, remembered lovingly.

It is written: *"I believed, therefore I have spoken. With that same spirit of faith we also believe and therefore speak" 2 Corinthians 4:13 (NIV)*

All Thanks be to God…

FOREWORD

Matthew 4:1-4 of the Bible tells the story of Jesus being tempted, saying, "Then Jesus was led by the Spirit into the wilderness to be tempted by the devil. After fasting forty days and forty nights, He was hungry. The tempter came to Him and said, "If You are the Son of God, tell these stones to become bread." But Jesus answered, "**It is written.** Man shall not live on bread alone, but on every word that comes from the mouth of God."

Much like Jesus, have you ever found yourself being tempted with the feeling of no escape? Have you ever questioned the identity of who you are in Christ or had it challenged by someone else? Have you ever been hungry and yearned for more than what this life seems to have offered you? If your response is "yes" to any of these questions, know that the answers you seek are encapsulated **in the written** Word of God.

Much like Jesus, you too have the power to overcome every snare and trap that the enemy has set in your path. For if you have an ear to hear, you will find that the precious gift of God's voice, leading and guiding you, can not only be found in the written verses of the Bible but also in other God-inspired readings like Rev. Yvette Y. Carter's new release, *It is Written… My Voice in Verses.* Filled with colorful stanzas, melodic rhymes, touching free verses, beautiful prose and soul-stirring figurative language, this book is an uplifting, poetic journey for the mind, heart, spirit and soul.

Much like me, a woman who is daily trying to find her own voice and write her own verse, I pray that as you read this masterful collection of poems, you will hear the melodic tone of God's voice and in doing so find the melody in your own! Be blessed by the readings, but more than anything, be open and allow the imagery, word association, musical qualities and language that Rev. Yvette Y. Carter offers to transform your life in such a way that you will be able to declare and decree out of your own mouth and without hesitation…it is written!

To Rev. Yvette Y. Carter, on behalf of all women who have benefited from your words and watching your journey, thank you for trusting God through this process and sharing more of yourself with us through this book.

Forever your friend, sister and God's servant, Rev. Sherita Holt.

PREFACE

I t was in 2015 when I realized and declared, I wanted to LIVE AT FULL VOLUME, creatively, as a writer, #1 best-selling author, minister of movement and song. I was having a good time with my sisters and our daughters, designing and deciding what we wanted to do and where we wanted to be on our 2015/2016 Personal Goals Vision Boards. I had been writing since before 2004, randomly and in unplanned moments, recording what was on my heart, in my spirit or requested for special occasions.

I knew that I was carrying something great within me that was not just for me. There was something to be shared that would uplift and encourage, bring light and love. My encounters with God and the revelations brought forth from those encounters could possibly change the world. It was time, so I began to organize what had been poured out through the pen.

I desire to be empty when I leave this earth with no regrets, having left behind a legacy of creativity, love and praises to God for the generations to come. In the words of Beyoncé, "I was here."

My Thoughts
&
Inspirations

May he be pleased by all these thoughts about him, for he is the source of all my joy. Psalm 104:34 (TLB)

Always have a song on your heart. God has done glorious things. Close my natural eyes that my spiritual eyes might be open to see what God has for me.

SELAH

(Matthew 26:40-46)
As a disciple for Christ, am I awake, or am I sleeping and resting away my time? Am I available to go and preach, dance and teach the gospel of the Lord? Am I asleep on Jesus, so He can't use me? Am I resting in the fact that someone else is staying awake and watching and praying? Am I sleep-walking? My eyes and ears are open, but what is getting in? Am I spending too much time watching TV, playing video/electronic games, working or worrying? Am I afraid to wake up for fear of what I might find? What will I really see—MYSELF? What will I really hear—GOD? What will I really feel—the HOLY SPIRIT?

Where will I be when Jesus comes looking for me? Will I be asleep, or will I be awake and ready to move?

SELAH

(Ezekiel 37:1-14)
Speak to your own dry bones. How can I go out and bring life to someone else when I am dead? Encourage yourself and know that there is nothing too hard for God. All things are possible with God. After the reconnection, there is a covering. There is protection.

10

SELAH

(Hebrews 4:13)
There is nowhere to hide. Nowhere to put away your sins. Nowhere to put away unforgiveness.

In our homes, we put our mess behind screens, under beds and in cabinets. There's nowhere like that to shield our stuff from God. EXPOSED!

SELAH

(Psalm 23:4)
Sometimes no matter what you want for yourself, God knows what's best for you. When you think you need to be up front, God says, "No, move to the back." When you think, *I got this; I'm not going far*, if you don't take God with you, you will die. God/Jesus/Holy Spirit is your safety belt.

Thank You, Lord, for a safe place. When I can't find my way, You find Your way to me!

SELAH

The middle—not the beginning, but not yet the end. In the middle, the place where you must decide whether to turn back or press forward. It's easy to go back or turn back to the familiar, but the blessing is pressing forward into the unfamiliar. Step forward in faith, believing that you are one step closer to better, knowing that the end is only a new beginning, trusting that God knows what's best for you.

SELAH

(Psalm 118:24)
This is the day that the Lord has made. What are you going to do with it?

ONE DAY AT A TIME
(MY DEVOTIONAL TIME WITH GOD)

...and if you will swear by me alone, the living God, and begin to live good, honest, clean lives, then you will be a testimony to the nations of the world, and they will come to me and glorify my name. Jeremiah 4:2 (TLB)

Pace Yourself

I have seen something else under the sun: The race is not to the swift or the battle to the strong, nor does food come to the wise or wealth to the brilliant or favor to the learned; but time and chance happen to them all.
Ecclesiastes 9:11 (NIV)

As I was driving in this morning, I found myself trying to keep up with or pass the other cars on the road. Not because I was late, but just because I could go as fast or faster. Then I was reminded of the scripture and I drove at my own pace. It's reckless to try and run your race at the same pace as others. You could end up pulled over (throwing off your timing and missing your blessing) or getting to the finish line and not having all you need to cross it, or you could crash and burn and never finish the race. Pace yourself because you win just by finishing the race!
Hebrews 12:1-3 (NIV), 1 Corinthians 9:24-25 (NIV)

#checkyourselfbeforeyouwreckyourself

The Lyrics of My Life

Sing to the Lord a new song; sing to the Lord, all the earth.
Psalm 96:1 (NIV)

Although the lyrics of my song may be the same as yesterday, I should be singing with a different attitude (of gratitude) today. Everyday we are given brand new mercies and another chance to change our lives and the lives of others. So, get a new song (attitude, outlook) and give God the glory.

14

Don't let the songs of the sway of the trees or the roar of the sea be all the praise that reaches God's heart, but let Him hear an original song written by your voice, your love, your worship, your praise! *#refrainfromcomplaining #liftyourvoice #tryingtogodeeperandhigher*

Keep Hope Alive

I will never forget this awful time, as I grieve over my loss. Yet I still dare to hope when I remember this: The faithful love of the Lord never ends! His mercies never cease. *Lamentations 3:20-22 (NLT)*

If things aren't good, they could be worse; if stuff is happening to you and you don't understand why, don't question it, but rejoice in knowing that God is still in control. He does all things well! When it looks like the enemy has won and you feel down for the count, can't get back up, thrown in the towel, waved the white flag—be reminded that if God be for you, who in all the world can be against you? It's temporary; this too shall pass, brand new mercies every morning, trouble don't last always! Keep your head up, stay prayed up, press in and press through! Be encouraged, my brother and my sister, and He will strengthen your heart if you yet hope in the Lord. Keep hope alive! Keep hope alive!

Blessed To Be A Blessing

This service that you perform is not only supplying the needs of the Lord's people but is also overflowing in many expressions of thanks to God. *2 Corinthians 9:12 (NIV)*

Yesterday, four generations came together to celebrate the dedication of a baby back to God. In that moment, I was reminded of the blessings in my life! What was offered to my parents was offered to me, we offered to our children, and our children have now offered the same to their children. It is our duty and responsibility to introduce our children to God. Teach them how to love God, their neighbors and themselves. Let us stop taking the blessings of God for granted! I challenge you to make your mark by being a blessing to someone else. Reach out to those who are lost, alone, hurting and feeling left out.

Navigating the Storm

And thine ears shall hear a word behind thee, saying, This is the way, walk ye in it, when ye turn to the right hand, and when ye turn to the left. *Isaiah 30:21 (KJV)*

In this life, we will travel to places that are familiar and unfamiliar. There is comfort in traveling to a familiar place because we already know the way. We may even know 2-3 different routes to get where we are going because of traffic, time, or distractions. There can be uneasiness in traveling to an unfamiliar place because we don't know the way. This is when we turn on the navigation/GPS or print out the MapQuest directions. We put in the destination and get turn-by-turn instructions. However, when a storm arises while we are traveling to a familiar or unfamiliar place, we can become disoriented and lose our way. There can be nothing worse than being lost in a storm. We can call someone on our cell phone, or pull over and wait out the storm, or we could allow GPS—*God's Positioning System*—to recalculate the route and get us going the right way to reach our destination safely. I challenge you today to allow God to lead you everywhere—work, school, home, church, life.

Giving God Your Best

For God so loved the world, that he gave his only begotten Son, that whosoever believeth in him should not perish, but have everlasting life. *John 3:16 (KJV)*

Have you given God your best today? Any day? Anytime? Did you do it because you expected something? We are born into this short life, which will be full of trouble (Job 14:1). We can choose to give God our best or give Him what's left. He gave us His best: His only Son. I have an only son, and I wouldn't be willing to give my only son for this sick and dying world. Whatever we do, do it as unto the Lord. Will it be pleasant? No, there will be some pain and pressure. The weight of it all will get heavy, and we will get tired. Push past the pain, pray past the pressure, praise your way through. I challenge you to give God your best—the best of your gifts and talents, your best offering, your best praise. At the end of the day, your press in, your press pass, will glorify God, edify the people of God and terrify the enemy of God.

Trusting God

I praise God for what he has promised. I trust in God, so why should I be afraid? What can mere mortals do to me? *Psalm 56:4 (NLT)*

We put our trust in man, and more times than not, we are disappointed, disregarded or dismissed (job, family, school, church). While we need to be in relationships with our fellow man, it's our relationship with Christ that gives us the wisdom, strength, patience, and peace we need to stay "checked in." God is the Promise Keeper. We can trust His promises always (Deuteronomy 31:8; Jeremiah 29:11). It's not going to be easy, but with God, all things are possible. I challenge you to live fearless, courageous and confident because of His promises. Every day praise God for who He is! Praise God because He is! Praise God because He will! Praise God just because!

Living by Faith

My eyes are always on the Lord, for he rescues me from the traps of my enemies. *Psalm 25:15 (NLT)*

How are we supposed to walk out this life if we are always looking up/around? We are sure to walk into/fall into something (walls, people, holes, dangers, temptations) if we are not watching where we step and keeping track of everything to the left and the right. It's not our physical eyes that are always on the Lord, but our mind and our heart. The Bible tells us "We walk (live) by faith (believing) and not by sight (seeing)" *2 Corinthians 5:7 (NKJV)*

So, I challenge you to keep your faith activated, allow the Holy Spirit to lead you and not only will the enemy's traps be avoided, but you can walk with God-confidence in the path He has set before you. It is my prayer that once we accept where God is taking us, we can rejoice on the way.

What's In Your Hand?

"For I know the plans I have for you," says the Lord. "They are plans for good and not for disaster, to give you a future and a hope." *Jeremiah 29:11 (NLT)*

Playing the hand I've been dealt...I see you and I raise a praise to God; stop bluffing and show your hand -- I've got a royal flush and I'm done gambling with all that's precious to me (family, values, good works, faith)!! You have to know when to hold and when to fold. Leave the table before all that you value (peace, joy, strength, growth, etc) is just chips in the other "players" pile. Walking away a winner!
1 Corinthians 7:20, Isaiah 30:21 (NLT)

Don't Believe Me -- Just Watch

Behold, I will do a new thing; now it shall spring forth; shall ye not know it? I will even make a way in the wilderness, and rivers in the desert. *Isaiah 43:19 (KJV)*

Don't believe me, but just watch God turn your mourning into dancing; from your pain, He'll give you power. In the midst of chaos, a peace that surpasses understanding. God is able to turn every situation around. That which the enemy meant for evil, He will make good. He will work all things out for your good and His glory. You don't have to stay in the state that you are in. God is always watching and working, healing, delivering and setting free. Try Jesus! Peace-giver, Joy-river, Way-maker! *Philippians 4:19 (KJV)*

#won'tHedoit #Iamatestimony

In the Midst of It

I will bless the Lord at ALL times; His praise shall continually be in my mouth. *Psalm 34:1 (KJV)*

When a diabetic does not eat correctly or every few hours, their blood sugar level can drop extremely low, causing a medical crisis. They can become disoriented, argumentative and helpless. It is very important for them to get something to eat as soon as possible to boost their blood sugar. (It was in the midst of his medical crisis—as argumentative and disoriented as he was—that I heard him say, "Praise God, bless the Lord; everything is going to be alright." In the midst of the crisis, he praised God. It was in that moment that God gave him the ability to describe where he was and allowed him to listen to the person on the phone.) Even when we don't know how to help ourselves or feel like we don't know where we are or what we are doing, praising God will always lead you to the help that is needed. Praise is a guiding light out of a dark situation!

Being a Champion

So, David triumphed over the Philistine with only a sling and a stone, for he had no sword. Then David ran over and pulled Goliath's sword from its sheath. David used it to kill him and cut off his head. When the Philistines saw that their champion was dead, they turned and ran. *1 Samuel 17:50-51 (NLT)*

You don't need to be the best at a thing; you don't need to be the strongest or the biggest or the fastest; you don't need to have an army of followers.

You only need that which you use day to day to be equipped to win – faith (the size of a mustard seed), the "proven" Word of God (in your heart), wisdom (gained from previous experience); prayer (without ceasing), a made-up mind and the assurance that if God be for you, who can be against you. Know that what God brings you to, He will bring you through! You win with Christ!!

#livingredeemed

Get Rich Quick

But my God shall supply all your need according to His riches in glory by Christ Jesus. *Philippians 4:19 (TLB)*

You have got to check this out! Want to know how to get rich quick? Well…say "YES" to Jesus! Invite Him into your heart today. Become joint heirs with Christ and have everything you need. Rich with joy (unspeakable), peace (surpassing understanding), favor (full with blessing) and prosperity (health and soul).

#tryJesus

I

LOVE IS...

*Love never gives up, never loses faith, is always hopeful,
and endures through every circumstance.
1 Corinthians 13:4-7 (MSG)*

**May these poems minister to the hearts of all who will say
I do.**

This Is My Now

For Shukriyyah and Salim (August 20, 2008)

Once upon another time,
We fell in love and all was fine.
High school sweethearts,
Is how it starts.
WOW! This was my now.

Went away to get education,
To our love pledged your dedication.
When you were done, you looked for me,
Said I was the one, down on one knee.
WOW! This was my now.

Then marriage vows we shared,
Into each other's eyes we stared,
Unaware of what the future held,
A much greater love would prevail.
WOW! This was my now.

The children born, our love was torn,
Priorities shifted, our love had drifted.
WOW! This was my now.

For 29 years, we were together,
Believed our love would last forever.
Ten years elapsed, and the winds of time
Have blown us back, hence this rhyme.
WOW! This is my now.

Our life together, it didn't stop,
We simply paused, put God on top.
As we reflect, we reconnect,
The seasons changed, our lives both blessed.
WOW! This is my now.

This time it's different, yet somehow the same,
Much wiser now, yet our love remains.
The children grown and on their own,
This time just us, yet not alone.
WOW! This is my now.

Your love is true, so again this "I do"
Elated and glad, I do it with you.
By the hand of God, I believe we're here
Not fate, but faith, you were worth the wait.
WOW! This is my now.

When You Would Say "I DO"

My firstborn Charde' (June 11, 2010)

My baby girl, where in the world, did the time go,
It blows my mind yo, 24 years ago,
It seems like only yesterday, they lay you in my arms.

Eight pounds of pink and cuddly; suddenly,
I was filled with awe at what I saw,
In how perfect you'd been created,
Elated that you were meant for us,
Your daddy and me, sent to be
A borrowed treasure, whose worth we can not measure;
I stroked your hair, counted your toes and fingers too,
So far away the day when you would say "I DO."

What to do with a girl like you, so sweet and kind;
It blows my mind,
You, blonde, blue-eyed and beautiful,
Who God used to bring light in and heighten our faith in
Him. The stares, the glares, and prolonged glances, chances
To enhance man's tunnel view.
I wiped your eyes the times you cried;
So far away the day when you would say "I DO."

I knew in time, in the back of my mind, a woman you would
Become. It's bittersweet to say the least.
How fast the time has passed.
Not so far away, the day when you would say "I DO."

Encore!

For Nikki and Olu on Your Wedding Day (October 2013)

Once upon a time before,
Eighteen years and four
I saw you on the field and to you my
Heart would yield

This was the time we would find
I'd be yours and you'd be mine
But sad to say, to our dismay
It wouldn't last, the moment passed

Once upon a time before
In the year 2k, we found and reignited
The spark that was a light in
Our heart – Encore!

Once upon a time before
We lived our lives on separate paths
Never expecting our present would
Become our past, at last

The span of time we were apart
Was in God's plan to prepare our hearts
And rearrange our life
Making you my husband and me your wife

Once upon a time before…Encore!

But Love...

Howard & Yvette's 30th Wedding Anniversary (July 12, 2014)

Roses are red, violets are blue
For all of my adult life I have loved you,
And a few of my teen years too

Thirty years of marriage, many more as friends
I don't take it lightly this milestone in life,
Most times unlikely

It wouldn't be true if I said to you
That it's all been easy breezy,
Times get tough and
We've been through some stuff
But love… is what holds us up

You are my friend, and love 'til the end
What God has done can be undone by no one

We are flesh of flesh and bone of bone
My touchstone, my heart, my home

We've raised our kids
Our lives we've lived
With little, with plenty, through full and
Through empty
But love…is what has held us up

II

ALONG
THE WAY

Whether you turn to the right or to the left, your ears will hear a voice behind you, saying, "This is the way; walk in it." Isaiah 30:21 (NIV)

May these poems speak encouragement and hope to all who have been called to ministry.

Elijah

For Shakira, my Friend (June 2007)

You came into this world
Sooner than expected
You couldn't wait to get here
Making it for some of us
Just a little hectic

But what we failed to see
Was you had the inside scoop
For you knew exactly
For God had given the plan to you

You have come into this world
With all its stress and strife
But the mantle that you wear
The one that's on your life
You will always handle with tender loving care

See, God is in control
And there's nothing we can do
But trust He knows what's best
And help you follow through

The doctors have said this and that
About your health and growth
Sometimes it makes us worry
We've even shed a tear
But then we watch and understand
That God has got them both

So, whose report do we believe?
Who has the final say?
When all is said and done, you see
God will make a way

Elijah, strong and funny
Elijah, small and true
Elijah, great and mighty
Elijah, through and through

The Face Of Faith

(December 2010)

This is a tale about a place I know
It's small yet large, with room to grow
Where faces are glad, making the enemy mad
People are kind; all sorts you'll find
There's joy and peace; lots of laughter
A place of release; if it's truth you're after

The Word of God, it's where we gather
We cry, we dance, and give Him reverence
Prayer and fasting; praise in His presence
We give each other hugs and kisses
Even phone calls when someone misses
Its fertile, purple, and been a blessing
Y'all still guessing, STOP – it's FTOPP
Faith Tabernacle of Prayer and Praise
A place where our voices we raise

This is a place where you'll find love
A place that fits you like a glove
Teaching, birthing and training
Reaching, preaching and praying

The CME's, accessible, addressable
Their feet firmly planted; Standing
Under the leadership of God-equipped
Faith filled; spirit yielded women of God
Going hard for the Lord
As for Pastor Vangie, Evangelist like none other

32

Friend, auntie, teacher, God-mother
Kimberly D Y, our Senior Pastor, word master
She's fly, got shine; but don't get it twisted
Gets deep with the word and keeps you uplifted

2010 the kind of year it's been
Had some pains and bore our crosses
Had some gains and experienced losses
Unemployment; redeployment; Dana, in glory,
Shouting "Present" to her name
Walking 'round heaven, legs no longer lame
Brothers Robert and Olu, Ms. Dee and Willette
And lest we forget, the return of Ms. Paulette

Give a hand to the band, shout out to those who
Dance; Men's chorus sang for us; Praise Team, y'all
Be singing, LEVITES a delight

Good teaching; great preaching; God reached in and
We heard a word- Jesus came to bring the fire;
Somebody ought to say thank you
Get in position for your transition; It's in your belly
It's destiny waiting to say I do; You can get with this
Or you can get with that; Bruised to be used; Can't
Keep a good man down; I am under construction; and
The inside man

Wherever you see us, we'll be praising Jesus
Bowling in Capital Plaza; as a presence at the park
By the water, doesn't matter, 'round the corner, up
The street, American Rescue Workers, we meet

Not enough time to tell it all; We've done much,
Big and small; We're not worried, glory in our sight
As we keep giving and trying to live right

Lord, in heaven, Thank God for 2011!

It's Time

For April, Young Minister in the Gospel (February 2007)

Before your birth, God knew your worth
Your gifts and talents, He'd sift and balance
And into His kingdom, bring them.
So, this day in motion, He did set
He's just got started, I've got a notion,
He ain't finished yet.

For this day, you have been prepared
So, don't be anxious, nervous or scared
For as God has declared, He is still in control
So April be bold in what the Lord has given
As toward this day you have been living.

Don't let anyone look down on you
Some may say at 21, she's just too young
Live your life beyond the strife, walk the walk
And talk the talk.
I'm so inclined to just remind you
Your age a stamp that does not define when
God says, "It's time, Boo!"

Your past, your present, that's your history
Your future no longer unknown, a mystery
No longer rely on your own understanding
For at times this calling will be so demanding
But the Word of God is tried and true
It is where you should look to bring you through

You'll make mistakes and that's expected
You've got what it takes, just stay connected
Your life is bright, a light in the dark
So, for the youth today go make your mark

I'm thrilled and filled with joy and
Glad to say, out loud, this day how proud
I am for what the Lord has done
I've watched you blossom and grow in grace
And I'm excited to see you take your place
So, dance and preach for an audience of one
And God will be pleased as will the Son

Now is your time divinely designed
Be strong and assured and not obscured
By the plan of attack from the enemy, for
The Father, Son and Holy Ghost, the three is one
And He's got your back!

Demon Slayer

For Pastor Kimberly (December 2009)

Yea high, 'bout four foot nine,
You're cool, yes, fly,
Elder Andre thinks you're fine.
You're smart, got heart
Been set apart.
Got skin of brown
Your voice you raise in praise
A song to sing
From no-one, from no-thing
Will you back down.
You're a wife and mother,
We love her, you're our spiritual cover.

Filled with His Word,
Teaching, preaching -- the gospel
You'd know, if you've heard or
Even just sit and talk a spell.
What more can we say 'bout this Woman of God?
There's just so much that we could applaud.
Of course, the applause you'd deny,
Give back unto God, you'd glorify.

Thanks for your labor on our behalf,
We pray for your favor as you journey this path.
The anointing you're under, the way God made ya,
No wonder you're dubbed the "Demon-Slayer."

The life you live, the love you give,
Is a testament to the investment
Of time spent before the Lord.
We pray this rhyme is evidence
Of what you've meant
To this three strand chord.
So, rest assured, we've got your back,
We'll pray, we'll fast, when the enemy attacks.

The Inside Thoughts Of Me

Written by Howard N. Carter, Jr. (December 2009)

People keep asking why is he so silent? I wonder if its 'cause
he lacks it?
Never stopping to ask him what is hurting.
Shut down, put down, now done acting.

Like what they say will never affect him
No friends, no family to protect him
Like no matter what he does, its
Not the best of him, so done saving the ones that
maimed him.

Tears running down, but still silent
No emotions left, it would seem they tamed him
But one day they'll fame him
Taking pictures, sailing and no longer nameless
He's a man.

Unbreakable, never again wavering
All he can muster is a wave at them
Bow his head and pray for them, that
One day they'll understand him
But until then he will stay far away from them.

III

PRECIOUS
BLESSINGS

Children are a gift from the Lord;
they are a reward from him.
Psalm 127:3 (NLT)

May these poems resonate with every mother everywhere.

I See You Lord

For my Niece Takia (April 2006)

In the smile on her face;
In the midst of her faith
I see You Lord

I see You in the breeze, as You whisper
Through the trees
I see You in the rain,
Through my trouble and pain
I see You Lord

When no one cares, and life gets hard to bear
And I'm left alone and unaware
I see You Lord

I see You when my baby kicks me
I delight in You when the enemy tricks me
And I fall into his trap, but You wrap Your loving arms
Around me In Your tenderness and the enemy is dismissed
I see You Lord

When I look at my belly, I know You are able
And I am ready to bring forth this life
Through labor with favor
I see You Lord

I thank You Lord for Your only begotten,
Jesus Your Son, who has not forgotten
The One who will help me

When I'm in need as I deliver
And raise this blessed male seed
I see You Lord

My body has changed, my mind is new
My life will never be the same and I have no shame
And it's all because of You, In Your name I pray
Every day I stay grateful, for You have been faithful
I see You Lord

When mom and dad gave all they had
And grandma gives her life advice
I see You Lord

When this is done, and I birth this son
You'll be the one
To whom praise I'll raise
Throughout my days
I see You Lord

Our Sugar And Spice

My Firstborn Charde' (December 5, 2008)

Our sugar and spice and all things nice,
Our baby girl came into this world.
She made us wait, she took her time,
My pain was great, but after,
Joy sublime!

Our sugar and spice and all things nice,
She lit up our life, all blonde and bright
Eyes of blue, what an awesome sight!
At first surprised, but not really you see,
I looked in her eyes,
when she looked back at me,
I came to understand,
That me and her dad,
We're only part of the plan that God had.

Our sugar and spice and all things nice,
The doctors in awe, people coming in
To get a peep.
She was beautiful and sweet,
Not unlike the others,
Except this time, I was really the mother!

Our sugar and spice and all things nice,
God had blessed us with someone special,
Not just her heart, but the outward vessel.

Our sugar and spice and all things nice,
Our albino baby, hair, eyes and skin
Alluring, appealing, to draw you in,
Love-filled and goodness within.
Beautiful, creative, shy or coy, full of joy
Inspired, intelligent, gifted and insightful,
Necessary life, altogether delightful.
Open, receptive baby girl
God's gift of tolerance to the world.

Our sugar and spice and all things nice
She is strong and weak, sour and sweet,
She has touched our lives in ways we can't speak
We taught her much, how to love and laugh
To look pass herself and embrace her path.

Our sugar and spice and all things nice,
Okay, so things were done out of order.
But God is good and this life He'll water.
'Cause we stopped by the altar and laid it down,
Leaving it up to God, it's in His hands now.

To our sugar and spice and all things nice,
Along with you, Tyree, I say
Seek God, Him please, pray
Humbly before Him on your knees.
It won't be easy-breezy, problem-free
With God in the midst, a blessing it will be.

Our sugar and spice and all things nice
No longer is she our baby girl
For in just a few weeks, into this world
She'll deliver their own baby girl
Their sugar and spice and all things nice.

IV

REASON FOR THE SEASON

"Don't be afraid, Mary," the angel told her, "for you have found favor with God! You will conceive and give birth to a son, and you will name him Jesus. He will be very great and will be called the Son of the Most High. The Lord God will give him the throne of his ancestor David. And he will reign over Israel forever; his Kingdom will never end!"
Luke 1:30-33 (NLT)

May these poems ignite the light of love for Christ Jesus in your heart.

The Perfect Gift

(December 2007)

It's not in a box, all wrapped and tied
It's not neatly folded and smoothed inside
Not a blouse, spouse, new car or house
These things are nice, but we pay the price

It's not because I was good or bad
Not because I'm on the list of the man in red
It's not checked twice
For naughty or nice

There's no gift receipt
I can't return it or take it back
Isn't pulled from a shelf or off a rack

But is that gift that can lift you from a fit of depression
Or the pit of oppression
It can renew and revive
Help keep us alive

There is no debt that lingers still
His life He gave and God's will fulfilled
The perfect gift, His presence reverence
Who would have 'thunk' it
Just what I wanted.

Jesus Frees Us

(December 20, 2008)

It was the night of His birth and out in the field
Where shepherds doing what shepherds will.
A star shone bright, then an angel appeared
And spoke to the shepherds, saying "have no fear
I have come with good news, for one and for all"
While a chorus of angels sang Hallelujah, y'all!
Your ears will be glad, overflowing with joy
For down in the town of David, behold
A lowly baby boy, born of a virgin, as had been foretold

The angels departed and went back to heaven
The shepherds said to one another, let us go see this thing
That has happened
They found the family, to the baby paid reverence
Then went from among them, spreading the word
Of all they had seen and what they had heard

No room at the inn, no place out of danger
Only a stable with hay in a manger
His name they'd call Jesus
The name which would free us

The baby was wrapped in swaddling clothes
As the wise men followed the star that rose
From the east, they came, a King to see
Robed in innocence and majesty
As they came to the place, where the baby lay
They knelt before Him to worship and pray

Bearing gifts, before Him, they doled
Out frankincense, myrrh and gold

I don't remember a tree with lights that shone bright
Only the animals lowing in praise that night.
The shepherds, the Magi and angels alike
Were all witness to the wonderful sight
He is the reason for the season
Merry Christmas, Jesus born on this day
Merry Christmas, Jesus to show us the way
Jesus! The One that frees us!

V

TGBTG!!
(To God Be the Glory)

All glory to Him who alone is God, our Savior through Jesus Christ our Lord. All glory, majesty, power, and authority are His before all time, and in the present, and beyond all time! Amen.
Jude 1:25 (NLT)

Give God the glory! May these poems take you into His presence.

The Most High

(March 2007)

The Most High God; Our Maker, Creator
The Lord of Lords, The One I adore
The One who's faithful, So I'm ever grateful

Your face have I sought
Thought I could not see
But is revealed in your grace and
Mercy towards me
In the smile of a child
Or the breeze through the trees
I reverence your presence and majesty

This spiritual being in flesh and blood
Is dry and parched, yearning after Your love
But I'm learning to quench my thirst with
Praise and with worship

To Him that is first
In the strife of my life
And in my time of distress
With every breath it's
You that I bless
You heard my cry and didn't ask why

TGBTG!! (TO GOD BE THE GLORY)

Your praise I raise throughout my days
I'm not ashamed as I lift Your name
To share and declare that You are there

On my lips await a song to sing
I sing to You my peace, my joy, my everything

When I am least, Your strength increased
How dare we think that praise is a choice
Whether or not we lift our voice

So be sure unless you stop and hold your breath
It is His will you praise Him still.

Choices

Free will – God's will
Always moving – Standing still
Choices

Love – Hate
Give – Take
Choices

Good – Evil
Walk – Faint
Death – Life
Sinner – Saint
Choices

In – Out
Believe – Doubt
Whisper – Shout
Choices

Heaven – Hell
Money – Master
Succeed – Fail
Choices

Worry – Pray
Stand – Fall
Sit – Dance
Nothing – All
Choices

Chaos – Peace
Light – Dark
Strong – Weak
Choices

Hot – Cold
Yes – No
Timid – Bold
Choices

Against – For
Order – Mess
Sink – Soar
Spirit – Flesh
Choices

Jesus – Satan
Friend – Foe
Open – Shut
High – Low
Choices

Win or Lose, I Choose.

Everything

(March 2010)

Everything I give to You
Everything I trust You to do
Everything is in Your will
Everything I give You still
Everything in You is good
Everything I give as I should
Everything in You is fine
Everything is Yours, not mine
Everything I give to You

Everything You can do.

Father

(June 2006)

I've come today to have my say
About the One whose seed I'm from
See early in the 'morn, on the day I was born
He had my heart, from the very start
See as I began to learn and grow, I came to know
He loves me most, so I hold Him close
He is so dear, He's never far, but always near

He picks me up when I fall down
He gives me joy amidst my frown
Around the town, He's always there
Right by my side and everywhere
On Him I depend, on Him I rely
For who can mend and satisfy

When I am hurt and feel alone
He offers comfort like I've never known
When I go astray and disobey,
He may grieve, but He won't leave
That's just His way

He's never absent, always present
Even in my past, my future He plans
With His very own hands
He's fed me and led me, shared and cared
In every situation, He's my inspiration
In my daily meditation dedication
I listen for His still small voice
That will give me that one true choice

He holds me and molds me
My life in His outstretched arms
So holy, He boldly keeps me safe from harm

You ask yourself who is the One of whom I speak
Who gives me strength when I am weak
The length of my days who I will seek
To lead and guide, from Him I cannot hide
No matter where, He'll find me there

Some may want to call Him Pop
Others stop and call Him Daddy, but gladly
I call Him by the name I reverence, because in His
Presence it is my preference, Father
Father, not a man that He should lie
But the One who loves me no matter why
Father, the One who cheers me on
As I run this lifelong race
I'm not that swift, I keep the pace
And surely I've won a place in His grace

So, on this day while we honor men
As wonderful as they can be,
Consider this, what if we bother to give honor
To the Father; Oh, what blessings we'll see

Just Allow...

(2005)

If you would just allow Me to be God in your life
Through your stress and your strife,
Then I will bless your life beyond measure
It would be My good pleasure.

If you would just allow Me to be God in your relationships
Through the ups and the downs,
I will save, mend, set free and deliver,
As My love abounds.

If you would just allow Me to be God in your finances
Through the debt and the lack,
I will make a way out of no way,
I will bring prosperity back.

If you would just allow Me to be God
Just hear My every word.
I will do what I said I would
For this you have heard.
For I know the plans I have for you
Not to break you down, but make you sound.

If you would just allow Me to be God, I will bring you
From wretched to righteous,
From pitiful to plentiful,
From bashful to bold.
From worthless to worthy,
From stagnant to stirring,

From stench to sweet smelling,
From distraught to determined,
From disturbed to delighted,
From sinner to sanctified,
From victim to VICTOR!

If you would just allow...

Where Is Here?

(June 2011)

A place of pain and pressure
A place of situations and circumstances
A place of necessary "nonsense"
A place of mess to miracle
A place of weakness to strength
A place of pandemonium to peace
A place of insane to sane
A place of incomplete to whole
A place of promise and prosperity
A place of greatness and gratitude
A place of beauty and bounty
A place of truth and triumph

Here in the presence of the Lord
In Your presence, I learn lessons
I seek Your peace, I feel You move
I quiver, You deliver
In Your presence
I believe, in reverence
In Your presence,
This is where You are benevolent
Here in the presence of the Lord.

VI

TROUBLE IN MY WAY

Though He slay me, yet will I hope in him. I will surely
defend my ways to his face.
Job 13:15 (NIV)

Be encouraged…trouble don't last always.

Trouble

God was chillin' in the heavenly place
When the angels came to show their face
Who also came, bringing up the rear?
None else than Satan, the one we fear
Fresh from roaming to and fro
Checking out the earth, you know
God said, "Satan, I've got a friend
A man named Job, good to the end."
Satan replied, "Yeah, I peeped him,
You keep him prosperous and protected."
God said, "Check this - he's yours, take
Everything he's got, except his life, touch not."
Satan said, "Bet," and came back to earth
This is when trouble for Job was birthed.

Down In The Valley

(July 2006)

I was down in the valley just walking around
and the shadow of death was what I found.
Fear, uh huh, I had no idea. I just wanted outta there.
But God told me, daughter not yet, not right now, the time is
not set.

I was down in the valley just walking about and the comfort
of the Lord was all laid out. My soul was sure but my mind
impure, my spirit was willing, but my flesh was chillin'.

I was down in the valley just walking around, I knew I was
there, but I didn't know where.
I knew not why, but I could still see the sky.

I was down in the valley just walking through, in a weakened
state, focused on a pitiful fate. The enemy sneaked in and flew
open the gate, for his impish friends to participate. Hopeless,
brought helpless, doom and gloom were close at hand,
self-pity and doubtful made a grand stand.

I was down in the valley just passing through, when the shadow
of death, took on a look anew. I no longer submitted to the
darkness of death, but gave in to the light of new life and was
blessed. I was drawn into the dawn of a new day rising. I was
moved to receive relief from the grief abiding.

I was down in the valley just walking around, praying and
fasting but my troubles still lasting, staying on my knees

saying, "please, God, please." While the enemy sifted, my heart was lifted, my destiny made clear, my purpose revealed.

My circumstance, a chance for destination restoration. I was found, not lost, no longer in a state of pause. My heart was cleaned, many valley lessons gleaned, and blessings received. My burden was slaughtered in a valley of water; my soul filled with glee, as I heard God speak, "now daughter, and I was released!"

911 – Emergency Run

(April 2006)

Let me tell you a story 'bout how I fell short, when I forgot whose I was and felt out of sorts.

See it was late one night when I got the call; She couldn't breathe and she started to bawl.
When the feeling was gone from her hands and her feet and she could no longer hear me and was feeling beat.
I tried to calm her, but to no avail; I thought I'm her mother, how can I fail.
I don't understand, why she's so upset, when we just left her and she was at rest.

Well I started to panic and started to dress and I didn't know how I would handle this mess, but in the midst of my distress, I said call 911!

But the One I should call, I don't have to dial,
He's always there in the midst of your trial.

So, I began to pray and intercede, my Father responded, quite quickly indeed. See I cried out for help. Felt heaven's embrace of loving protection, that place of warmth and true affection, the help that keeps us from shame and humiliation.

See Jesus is my 911, He's able to make the emergency run; He'll come unimpeded and provide the help needed. He will show up with urgency....son.

Well, when it was over, and the drama was done, it was made clear to me that He was the One
That calmed the situation and stopped the frustration and held off the devastation.

See He is the Saviour in whose favor I walk and of whose promise I talk.
He is the one that is worthy
So, I pledge my life to love and to serve thee.

I thank Him for His intervention and by the way, did I happen to mention
That it's not that I love Him, but that He first loved me.
So, come to the cross, try Him and see
He'll turn you around and make your mind sound;
So, when your life's in a spiral and your heart is in denial, if you look to the hills there is your help.
So, call on Jesus, the true 911,
He'll come and make that emergency run.
He won't get lost or be delayed; don't be dismayed,
He will show up with urgency....son.

I'm Always There

(March 2007)

When others walk away, and it seems no one cares
In your situation, your challenges, each and every day
I'm always there

You may not see Me; maybe you don't hear
My still small voice
I'm always there

When the world forsakes you
And the enemy overtakes you
I'm always there

When all seems lost
And you can't find your way
I'm always there

When the bills are high
And dough is low
Just trust and know
I'm always there

When family has walked away
And they've gone astray
Remember this, I'll make a way
I'm always there

There is nothing and no one
That can keep Me from you
If you abide in Me and I in you
I'm always there

69

Not just for a season
I don't need a reason
You are My child,
Not because of your style
But because you are My first love
I'm always there

I'm not evasive nor elusive
There are no excuses
For why My name you don't speak
Or My power you don't seek
I'm always there

I'm always there
In your breath
In your strength
In your joy
In your peace
In your power
In your weak
In your sadness
In your madness
I'm always there
Forever to care.

Still Here

(October 2007)

Despite your circumstance and every chance
The enemy grabbed to kill your joy and make you sad
Still Here

For every defeat, a victory won
By the power of God and Jesus the Son
Still Here

You've suffered long and endured much
But by the Hand of God and His loving touch
Still Here

You knew the Father in your time of pain
And season of strife, you blessed His name
He blessed your life with peace abiding and joy residing
Still Here

Your life you've lived by love and grace
Some stumbling blocks while running the race
But in the midst of your fall, you surrendered all
Still Here

No mountain too high that faith won't move,
No valley to low that grace won't prove
Into the refiner's fire, ragged and tired,
Burning away the old to bring forth pure gold
Still Here

In all you go through, when your faith is true
And your worship pure, there's nothing you can't endure
Still Here.

71

I Thirst

(April 2004)

Lord, I thirst
Saturate my life with Your Holy Spirit

Lord, I thirst
Drench my home with Your peace that passes understanding

Lord, I thirst
Fill our churches with an overflow anointing

Lord, I thirst
Open up the floodgates and pour out Your safety and protection over my children

Lord, I thirst
I thirst for You, the true and living water. The spring of the waters of life, my cleanser,
My purifier, the One that washes me white as snow.

Lord, today I surrender my dry, parched, windblown life to You. Today I surrender in obedience to my thirst for a closer walk with Thee.

VII

TRANSFORMED

Don't copy the behavior and customs of this world, but let God transform you into a new person by changing the way you think. Then you will know God's will for you, which is good and pleasing and perfect. Romans 12:2 (NLT)

God's word goes from your head to your heart. May you be changed in every way.

More Than Meets The Eye

(December 8, 2009)

I'm more than meets the eye, listen closely I'll tell you why
I'm hurt and pain, healed in Jesus name, see

I'm more than meets the eye, look closely and you'll see why
I'm war and peace, where grace and mercy meet

I'm more than meets the eye, take my hand, I'll show you why
I've won, I've lost, but Jesus paid the ultimate cost

I'm more than meets the eye, I was bound, now free
Jesus getting up from the ground loosed me

I'm more than meets the eye, I'm joy and sorrow
Because of Him who holds tomorrow

I'm more than meets the eye, I'm famine and plenty
He's more than enough, He stands in gently

I'm more than meets the eye, I'm heart and soul
I'm Holy Ghost bold

I'm more than meets the eye, I'm despair and hope
In His inheritance I share, with the blood I can cope

I'm more than meets the eye, not just what you see, but
What is unseen, for what you see is not all that I'll be,
Transforming daily, I'm so much more -- I'm possibility!

Under The Influence...

(August 19, 2009)

Under the influence...
Worldly pleasures and such,
Earthy treasures, can't get enough
Led astray, day to day, out of touch
Tarnished spirits, jaded minds
Sinful living of all kind

Under the influence...
The almighty dollar, big baller
Shot caller, hey, cash and bling,
Honey, money is nice, cuz it gets me ice
But what's the price for glitter and gold
If when it's done in the end I lose my soul

Under the influence...
My pain and strife,
My choices, people's voices
Cursing God for this life, Dang G,
Man, this me, where's my peace,
Grace and Mercy?

Under the influence...
Over indulgence
Liquid courage, smoking, doping
No hope in what's real
'Cept how I feel - whether
Tethered and shot, popped or dropped
Overeating, abuse, misuse, can't overcome
Too numb

Under the influence…
Me, myself and I
It's all about me, cuz I'm fly
Don't need nobody, no help, I'm cool
Inconsiderate, selfish, fool

Under the influence…
Shame and guilt
Hiding and diving behind a wall I've built
Misguided, undecided, guarded, faint-hearted
Self-esteem low, unworthy at best
My life a total mess

Under the Influence…
When I'm In His presence
I reverence, His name,
No pain, no shame, guilt or strife
He paid the price for my sinful life
I'm changed, sustained
Heavenly gifts I gain

Under the influence…
Of God the Father, Son and Holy Spirit
Listen, listen can't you hear it?
"Yesterday is history"
"Tomorrow a mystery"
"Today is a gift" meant just for you
It's your present, up to you what you do!

Who Me?

(October 2006)

The one called misfit, unfit to be loved
Misunderstood and to the side been shoved
I've been told, yeah, but they can't mean me
That I'm made fearfully and wonderfully?

Who Me?
The one I see; myself on the 'just so' shelf,
Why I'm here, I'm not so clear
Afraid and scared, bruised and beat,
Cast out, talked about, sifted as wheat
Pray you say, God doesn't care
'Cause the devil is busy
Laying on layer by layer

Who Me?
Not the brightest, not the best,
Of no interest to the rest,
Not even beautiful, viewed as pitiful,
My life so plain, no fortune, no fame
My name, my shame;
I can't explain, why I remain.

Who Me?
It seems my life has no direction.
Amidst the mess and imperfection
I'm judged by my 'hood' and deemed no good
A reflection of my mom's and pop's one night conception
Rejection and disconnection to real affection

Who Me?
I'm convinced in order to cope that dope is my hope
My body, my worth,
My mind concealed;
I'm tossed aside, no truth revealed

Who Me?
Yes, you; the one I claim, the one created to revere My name
Through test and trial and every frustration
Has gained wisdom untapped and quiet
revelation.

Who Me?
Yes, you; the one for whom I love and care
No matter what, no matter where
Your complexion has no face in the value I place
On the way I love you and My warm embrace
It's not about your body type – uh, don't believe the hype
Your shape, your size, means nothing in My eyes
I see where you've been, I see you now
I know your future; I know where you're bound

It might be hard and even terrible, but
You've come this far, and it's been bearable
Look beyond your past and past your present
To the gift of a future in eternal pleasance
See, it's true what's been said, about how you're created
When the world's against you and your life debated
Understand and know, don't be afraid
The price was paid, your sin relieved
Trust in God and then believe
You have been made fearfully and wonderfully!

Because of Faith

(September 2004)

Am I willing to be faithful even unto death?
Can I be distressed and not destroyed?
Can I be shaken and yet stand?
Even when it looks bleak
Even when it looks like I can't make it through
Even when my strength is failing
Even when I'm worn, weary and weak
Even when there is no peace
Even when there is no hope, and I can't cope
When all else has failed
I can look to the hills towards my help
I can stretch my hands to the heavens
I can stand and wait
I can stand and wait
I can stand and wait
Even unto death,
Because of my faith.

Promise to Possession

For Set Free By the Word (August 2007)

Pastor Alinda tells me God has spoken
And this season for you, He has chosen
To take to a higher and deeper plane,
To praise and magnify His Holy name.

The journey may seem long, so
On your heart keep a song, be strong
Don't murmur and make complaint or faint
God never said, Saints, this would be easy, believe me,
So please be alert for this time will be worth
The place of more with overflow for sure.

The enemy, at large, but not in charge
Is roaming to and fro, he's listening, seeking
Slicking and tricking, hitting high and low
Yes, he'll attack to distract, but rest in the fact
If on your knees you pray, in His will you stay
Then you can say the enemy's defeated and
He'll have to beat it.

Don't let your situation, become a complication
In your blessed transformation
Be encouraged, not discouraged
Rise out of your pit, the time has come
There's work to do and a race to run
The pace you set, it doesn't matter
Forget the former and look to the latter.

You may run quick and even swift
And others you may pass, but
Be quite sure it's not how fast
That you can run, but it's if you endure after the gun.

Hold up the blood-stained banner, of the only master planner
Whose outstretched hand to this wretched man, can take us
From disaster into our promised land.

God has promised, He's made a vow
Now, just be patient, He'll show you how
To move from promise to possession
A time of press and learning lessons
You'll learn to wait, activate your faith
In order your turn to appreciate.

From promise to possession
That will be your lesson
From glory to glory
That will be your story.

Thank You Lord

(May 2006)

Thank You Lord, every day,
Thank You Lord that's what I say
In every way, I thank You Lord.
That's what I pray when the day is long
And I've lost my song and I'm caused to pause
And say Thank You Lord, anyway.

Thank You Lord, for Your protection
Your tender kindness and loving affection,
I thank You Lord, for keeping me connected
To the resurrected One who is the Son in whom I'm reflected.

In the light of day, I might see my way,
Just the same as in the dark of night.
I walk by faith and not by sight.
Thank You Lord, when the world's a threat, see
You reach right down and come and get me.

Thank You Lord God Almighty
For You're gentle handed
When we take for granted
The air we breathe and what we believe.

Thank You Lord, for food and shelter
When all the land's in helter-skelter.
Thank You Lord, for everything
For every ring of the telephone
For all the things inside my home.

Thank You Lord, my Shalom,
For Your Holy Spirit
For the peace so loud, only I can hear it.

Thank You Lord God, for I am blessed
And I am grateful that when I'm faithless, You are faithful.

I thank You Lord for all I've got,
The kids, the man, all of whom I love a lot.

Father God in the midst of it all, even when I fall,
You hear my call and the pain I feel, I know is real
But Your loving touch causes me to kneel
And reveal
My thanks unto You Lord.

Thank You Lord, for You're the One who is King of Kings
My everything in whom I trust
My heart might burst with the love You give as long as I live
I thank You Lord.

VIII

UNDER THE SUN

The thing that hath been, it is that which shall be; and that which is done is that which shall be done: and there is no new thing under the sun. Ecclesiastes 1:9 (NIV)

Every moment under the sun is precious. Look for God and listen for the voice of God. Be encouraged.

When He Speaks...

Inspired by the Beach in Aruba (September 27, 2010)

He spoke to the waters saying you can only come this far
They obeyed, thought it not bizarre

He spoke to the wind and the waves "peace be still" and
They obeyed His will

He spoke to the sun to rise and the moon to hide
And they complied

He spoke to darkness and the light
And they took their place as day and night

He spoke to the birds to fly and fish to swim
Everything obeys His every whim

When He speaks to me
Will I be like the waters and know
Where to cease and when to flow

When He speaks to me
Will I be like peace and be released

When He speaks to me
Will I be like a bird and take flight
Going in Him to higher heights

When He speaks to me
Will I be darkness or light
To someone else's life

86

When He speaks to me
Will I be like the fish and swim
Or sink not trusting in Him

When He speaks to me
Will I answer, will I move
Will I miss the chance and lose

When He speaks to me
How will I know
My thoughts will cease and I will go

When He speaks to me
What will I say
I'm not sure or Lord, have your way

When He speaks, I'll bow
When He speaks, I'll follow
When He speaks, I won't resist
When He speaks, I'll know my life He's kissed

Winds Of Change

Inspired by the Winds at the Beach in Cancun, Mexico (May 2007)

The winds of change blowing over the ashes of my past, sweeping through the pain of my life.
The strife and the struggles that I claim as my own, understanding they help define who I've become. I'm not alone, they can't melee or outweigh what I can accomplish or complete, by the power of the Spirit that is alive and thrives inside of me.

Winds from the east, the sunrise of the hope that the Lord is most high and His eyes on me fixed as my life He has kissed. The winds from the west, the setting of that which was and shall never be, and what is to come will be best for me.
The winds from the north and from the south, in the mouth of whose storm and rain I might be worn with pain. I may bend, but will not bow, knowing that my own self-worth will be the birth of how I will endure until the end when the Lord over my life a rainbow endows.

When bliss is amiss, and sorrow my tomorrow, I call on Him that rushes in and blows it over, and fills me up with joy unspeakable, the kind the enemy finds unreachable.
The winds that change and rearrange, the building tear down, but the foundation remains.
The winds that lift and sift away anything not firmly planted, lost or stranded.

The winds that change my pain to power; cause the seeds of my faith to bloom and flower.
The winds that change my restraint to release, to make me free;

My boundary to breakthrough, my crisis to confidence as I submit and repent, my tears to triumph as this race I run.

The winds of change beneath my wings so that I can soar, above discontent, disappointment, and so much more.
The winds of change that whisk the waves across the sands of time and thoughts in my mind to cleanse, to mend and purify. The winds that bring waves of light, that brighten the darkness, that washes over the shores of my existence, light that cleanses, transforms, renews; bringing with it a refreshing dew, so the enemy's plans and schemes askew.
The winds of change that blow against the grain to a place of spiritual growth and overflow.

In That Moment

(July 2009)

In the early 'morn, but still the dark of night
Amidst the blended sea and sky,
There was one lone star that shone bright
I know there were others, but they were hidden from sight
In that moment, I had no questions
Nor did I wonder why

People were walking along the shore
While the stars of night grew less and
The sun of day shone more
The waves, as they came in
Their rhythm the same, all night,
All day they didn't change
In that moment, I had no questions
Nor did I wonder why

The sky in shades of red, yellow and blue
With hints of white peeking through
The horizon was endless
As the sky touched the sea
The dolphins at play
While God you had your way
I felt close to you, as your daughter,
Just me, myself and I
In that moment, I had no questions
Nor did I wonder why

As I stand in the sand, my bare feet
Sinking into creation, feeling connected and complete
With the Father of nations
The sound of the waves, at a roar
Being silenced by the beauty of the breaking of day
The sun was awaking, a glow of golden rays
The birds in their element
Soaring above with elegance in the sky
In that moment, I had no questions
Nor did I wonder why.

Free

(August 2006)

Am I free? Who me?
Do I even understand the concept of liberty?
Am I bound
Am I stuck? Is my life in a rut?
When I think of His goodness
I know He has blessed, but still I feel tied to the mess
Of my death in the bondage of oppression and misconception.

Free? Who me?

If God be for me, who can be against me?
No enemy can overtake me,
For God won't forsake me
More than a conqueror
Who me?
With all my sin and iniquity
Yet, You still love me
Bet! I am FREE
Yes, me.

IX

ADAM'S RIB

And the Lord God caused a deep sleep to fall upon Adam, and he slept; and he took one of his ribs, closed up the flesh instead thereof; And the rib, which the Lord God had taken from man, made he a woman, and brought her unto the man.

And Adam said, This is now bone of my bones, and flesh of my flesh; she shall be called Woman, because she was taken out of Man. Genesis 2:21-23 (KJV)

Be empowered. May these poems inspire and uplift.

Woman Of Destiny

(February 2008)

Woman of destiny
God created from man asleep
With a rib from his side
He made us
Unique and fragile, strong and weak
Beautiful, tender, loving and deep

Woman of destiny
Sister, mother, giver of life
Daughter, friend, auntie, niece, faithful wife
We are many, not just in number
Some of us skinny, others plumper
Some of us tall, some are small
Petite and sleek, bold and meek
A rainbow in shades of browns and tints
Bronze, caramel and chocolate mint

Woman of destiny
The power we yield cannot be measured
So why aren't we loved, respected and treasured
We're abused, misused, beaten and bruised
Low self-esteem and disrespect our muse
Understand, no man can hold us down
But our low self-worth is what keeps us bound
See we fall prey to what others think
When instead we should pray and from our own cup drink

Woman of destiny
We're not defined by the twist of our walk
The sweet when we talk
The broad of our hips, the full of our lips
The sound of our voice, when it dips and rises
The soft of our touch or the love in our eyes, its
Not the soul in our feet that make us complete

But the secret of our strength lies silent within
'Til the situations of life make us shout aloud
With power from a pen
Or a song from our belly, sang again and again
Or the dance from our soul that cries out
Lord, make me whole

Don't let man define you or bind you
To your past, but reach beyond your limits
Don't lose precious minutes

Show forth your true woman
With class and finesse
Hand crafted by the very best

Woman, your purpose awaits
Shift into gear and bust through the gates
The time has come, declare today
I'm changing lanes, moving in faith,
Striving to be what God has called me
Woman of Destiny.

"S" On My Chest

(June 2017)

Not a Superwoman; no super strength or speed,
But, there is a power that supersedes;
Supernatural power of the blood; Grace and mercy,
Unconditional love
Draws us out of the muck and mire of our deepest
Distress, impressed with an
"S" on my chest.

SINNER
I fall short, out of sorts
Outside His will, He loves me still
Being tricked and tried, cleansed of all my sins
Penitence, deliverance, blessed
"S" on my chest.

SEED
In fertile ground, been implanted
Watered, tilled and roots engrafted
Growing, flowing into the light
Promise filled, blooming brightness
"S" on my chest.

SERVANT
Reliable, pliable with every breath
Flexible and fearless
Being stretched
Each day shedding tears less
Despite my mess, SOS

Seeking a Savior, God's favor
Feeling blessed
"S" on my chest.

SAVED
By His grace, He rescues me
Defeated, the enemy that bullies me
Strong in my weakness; bold in my meekness
Stepping into my destiny
Captured my heart and sensitivity,
No regrets, satisfied
Original, one of a kind
Peace rules my mind, no stress
"S" on my chest.

ABOUT THE AUTHOR

Yvette Y. Carter is a poet and sonneteer, a lyricist of sorts. This body of work came from her intimate time with God and the result of His sweet presence. Yvette is a native of Washington, D.C. She received her early education in the District of Columbia public schools and pursued higher learning at the University of the District of Columbia and Howard University, where she studied Engineering. Yvette soon discovered that becoming an engineer was not her "thing." She decided to pursue an opportunity to continue in federal service at the Environmental Protection Agency, where she worked for 37 years until retirement in January 2015.

Yvette has been married to her amazing husband for 36 years. This union blessed them with three children who produced her next generation: 14 grandchildren. Yvette enjoys shopping, dancing, and spending time with her family and close circle of friends. In June of 1992, Yvette ran into the outstretched arms of Jesus and dedicated her life back to Him. When you get a chance, ask her what made her run—she will be glad to share this with you.

Y vette accepted the call to ministry in 2003; shortly after, she was licensed to preach the gospel and was later ordained in 2008.

Yvette is a preacher, teacher, poet and praise dancer. She has served in various ministries and positions, including Church Administrator, Director of the Women's Ministry and Worship Leader. Yvette loves everything about the creative arts, especially when it can be expressed in worship. Yvette is thankful to God for His sufficient grace and enduring mercy.

"All that I am and all that I am not (yet), it is my desire to glorify His name with my whole life."

IT IS
WRITTEN...
MY VOICE IN VERSES

A POET'S PERSPECTIVE